Why Can't Humans Fly?

Contents

Written by Sarah Fleming   Illustrated by Wes Lowe

Collins

Why can't humans fly?

Birds are the right size and shape to fly.

feathers

wings

hollow bones

This bird is too big to fly.

Humans are *not* the shape or size to fly. We don't have wings. To have big enough and strong enough wings we'd need big and strong enough muscles to flap them. To have big enough muscles we'd need to have HUGE chests that stuck out more than a metre.

Even if we were shaped to have wings, we couldn't fly unless we changed in other ways. For a start, we're too big and heavy. Like birds, we'd need to make our bones hollow to be light enough to fly.

Just adding wings wouldn't allow us to fly. We'd need to change our bodies too.

light, sleek head to fly into wind

huge chest for muscles to flap wings

light, hollow legs

tight, sleek clothes to fly fast

Our shape and size controls what we can and can't do.

3

Size and shape

Animals come in lots of different shapes and sizes. Some animals use their size or shape to help them to survive.

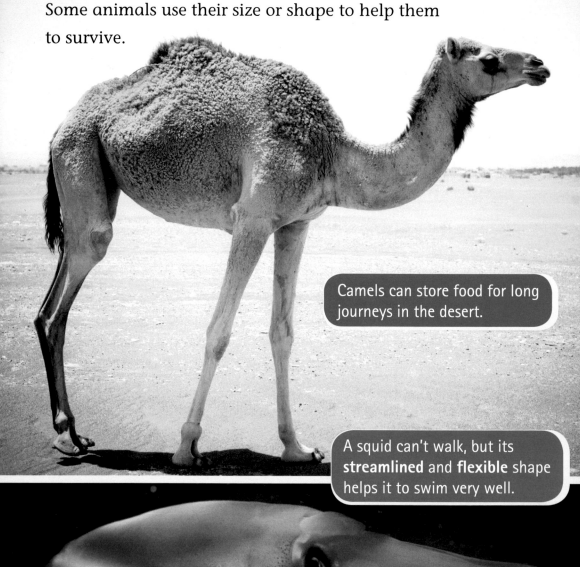

Camels can store food for long journeys in the desert.

A squid can't walk, but its **streamlined** and **flexible** shape helps it to swim very well.

Giraffes live in the African **savannah**. They compete for food with other leaf-eaters, like antelope. The advantage of having a long neck is that a giraffe can reach food that others can't.

Tiny pond skaters can walk on water to catch fallen insects.

Female peacocks want to mate with the biggest and best male they can find. This is so that their babies will be bigger and less likely to be attacked. So male peacocks have big tails to attract a mate.

The male peacock's tail lifts and opens up to attract a mate.

An amoeba has only one cell. It doesn't have guts, eyes or anything much. It's so small that it doesn't have to breathe or eat. Enough food and **oxygen seep** through the cell wall for an amoeba to live.

This wouldn't work if it got any bigger. Amoebas *have* to be small to live the way they do.

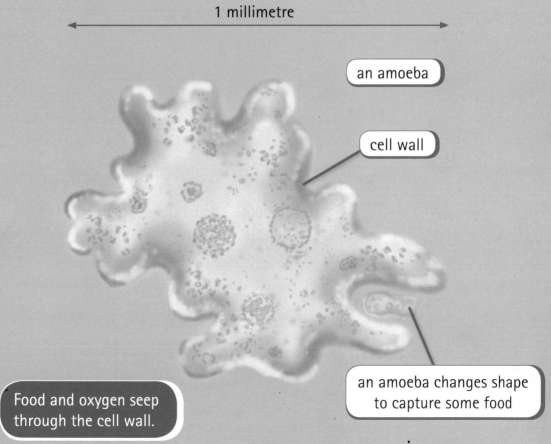

1 millimetre

an amoeba

cell wall

an amoeba changes shape to capture some food

Food and oxygen seep through the cell wall.

By being different sizes and shapes animals can live together in a **habitat**. They might eat different foods, sleep in different places and live in different parts of the habitat. But they are all the right shape and size to live in their special place in their habitat.

Why can't insects be dog-sized?

Insects have special places in lots of habitats. Their shapes are different, but they can't get bigger. This is because insects don't breathe in and out. Air seeps in through holes called **spiracles**. It flows round branching tubes, and muscles take in the oxygen in the air. The air seeps back out again.

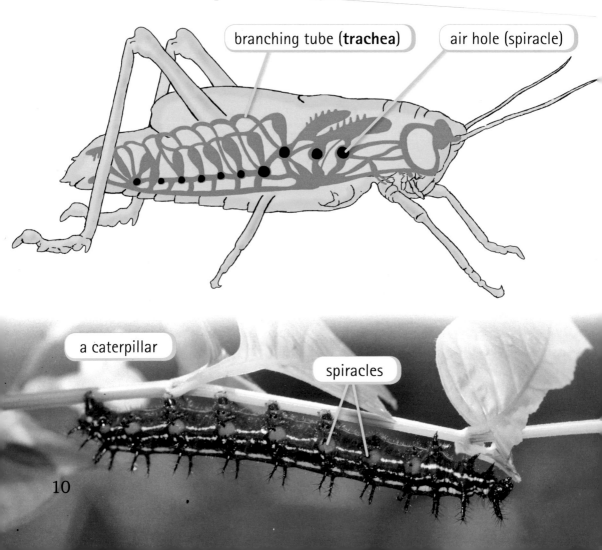

branching tube (**trachea**)

air hole (spiracle)

a caterpillar

spiracles

Oxygen can't flow very far down a trachea. Bigger insects couldn't get enough oxygen and would die. This way of breathing limits the size of insects.

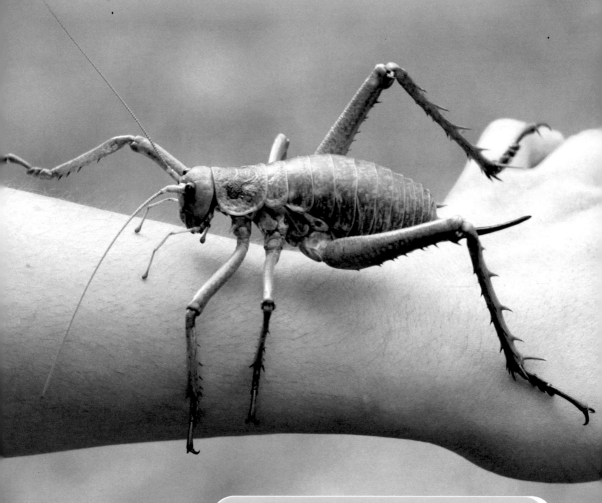

Even this huge insect has to have a thin body so that oxygen can seep all the way inside.

Insects are small, which for them is an advantage, because they survive on things larger animals aren't interested in. There are other advantages to being small.

Why are ants so strong?

An advantage of being small is that you can be strong. It's easier to lift your **body weight** if you're very light.

As animals get bigger, their weight increases much more than their strength. A muscle that is twice the size of another muscle is *not* twice as strong.

Like most insects, ants are mainly made of muscle. Human bodies are full of bones and organs like brains and lungs. In fact, humans are only about 40% muscle.

Leafcutter ants can lift 50 times their own body weight. The strongest humans can't lift even four times their own weight.

13

Why can fleas jump so far?

Another advantage of being small and light is that you can be shaped to jump a long way.

Fleas are the best jumpers on the planet. They can jump 200 times their body length. There are two reasons for this:

● Fleas are almost completely made up of muscle. For every gram of weight, there is a lot of muscle to help them to jump.

● Fleas have a "spring" coiled above their back legs which helps them to jump.

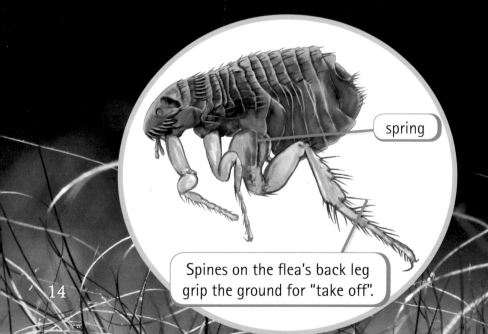

spring

Spines on the flea's back leg grip the ground for "take off".

Humans are heavier than fleas
and less of our weight is muscle,
so we can't jump very far at all.

Why can't elephants jump?

Compare a flea with an elephant. A little, light flea can jump easily. An elephant might just be able to leap over a ditch, but it can't jump upwards.

Most animals jump upwards by bending their legs first so that they can spring up. An elephant can't do this. Its legs are short, strong and very thick. They're the size and shape they are to carry its huge weight – about the same weight as 80 people. Because of their shape they can't bend enough to make a "spring" strong enough to jump.

Elephants don't need to jump – they can push down trees, travel long distances and swim. And because they're so big they don't have many **predators**. So for them, being large is an advantage.

Why can bears live through a polar winter and flies can't?

When it's cold, being big is also an advantage.

Big animals like polar bears can stay warm. They have lots of thick fur to trap heat and are also big enough to carry a thick layer of fat (up to 10cm thick) under their skin.

Flies are too small to carry fat to keep warm and they have no fur. They get very cold.

Many animals move to warmer places, but flies die in the winter cold. Their eggs survive and hatch in the spring.

a fly hatching

caribou escaping the winter cold in Alaska, USA

Why do whales live longer than shrews?

Another advantage of being big is that you live longer.

Animal	Length or height of animal	Can expect to live:
Blue whale	30 metres long	80 years
African elephant	3.7 metres tall	70 years
Monitor lizard	2.1 metres long	15 years
Shrew	5–8 centimetres long	1–2 years
Mayfly	0.5–0.8 centimetres long	30 minutes to one day

Big animals tend to live at a slower pace than small ones – an elephant plods slowly, whereas a shrew scurries quickly. An elephant's heart beats 30 times a minute, while a shrew's heart beats 800 times per minute. You age with every heartbeat, so a shrew gets old much more quickly than an elephant.

A shrew burns energy so quickly that it has to eat its own body weight every day.

Some animals don't follow this rule. Usually they are small animals that move very slowly and have a slow heartbeat.

Galapagos turtles move slowly and have a slow heartbeat. They can live up to 180 years.

What about us?

We humans live much longer than we should, when you think of our size. A healthy human today can expect to live up to 90 years – longer than a whale.

500,000 years ago our **ancestors** lived for about 20 years. They had lots of predators, illnesses, **famines** and battles, which cut life short.

So, what's changed? Our bodies – especially our brains – **adapted** over time. We stood up, got bigger and became cleverer. Adapting to survive better is called evolution.

We learnt how to make fire, use tools and talk and we started living longer. As well as adapting our bodies, we are the only animal that has adapted our habitat. We have invented medicines to keep us healthy, clothes and houses to keep us safe, warm and dry. All these things have helped us to live longer.

We even invented a way to fly.

Evolution

Humans aren't the only ones who have adapted over time.

The scientist Charles Darwin first said that animals changed
and adapted to their habitats.

When he looked at types of small birds on an **isolated** island,
he found that each had a different-shaped beak. They had
adapted the size and shape of their beaks so that they didn't
compete with each other for food. Each type of beak was adapted
for picking up different types of seed.

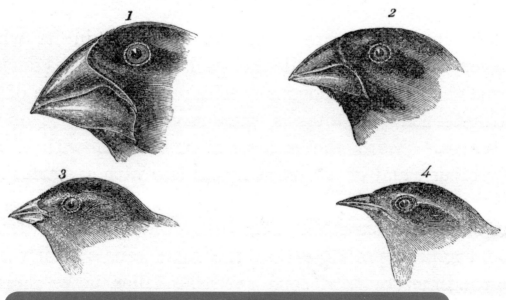

sketches made by Darwin of different beak shapes in the 1830s

Horses were the size of dogs 55 million years ago. They were small enough to duck and hide in their forest habitat. Over time, the climate changed and the forests became grassland. Horses adapted by becoming bigger so that they could travel faster and over longer distances.

a horse 55 million years ago

a horse today

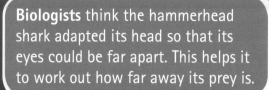

Biologists think the hammerhead shark adapted its head so that its eyes could be far apart. This helps it to work out how far away its prey is.

eye

eye

The stick insect's shape is a kind of **camouflage**. It confuses predators.

Some animals have not needed to adapt for a long time. Crocodiles have not changed since Tyrannosaurus Rex lived, 65 million years ago. By then, crocodiles had already adapted to their habitat so well that they stopped changing. They had adapted to be strong, fast and sleek and they had no predators.

a fossil crocodile from 65 million years ago

a crocodile today

Most animals continue to adapt to survive better in their habitat, or to fit into a changing habitat. This goes for humans too. As the Earth changes around us, we need to evolve and change so that we can be the best size and shape to suit our world.

Glossary

adapted	changed over time to fit a new purpose
ancestors	family members who lived in the past
biologists	people who study the science of living things
body weight	the heaviness of a person or animal
camouflage	a way of hiding things by making them look like something else
famines	not enough food, leading to people and animals dying of hunger
flexible	bends easily
habitat	the natural living place of an animal or plant
isolated	a long way from other places or people
oxygen	one of the gases in the air that living things need in order to stay alive
predators	animals that hunt other animals for food
savannah	a grassy plain in a hot country, with few trees
seep	flow slowly through, or into or out of something
spiracles	holes on the side of an insect that let air into its body
streamlined	shaped for easy movement
trachea	a tube in a body, which oxygen and other gases pass through

Index

Size, evolution and habitat

Why can't humans fly?

Birds are the right size and shape to fly.
Humans are *not* the shape or size to fly.

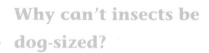

Why can't insects be dog-sized?

The way insects take in oxygen limits their size.

Why are ants so strong?

It's easy for an ant to lift its own body weight because the ant is very light.

Why can fleas jump so far?

Fleas are almost completely made of muscle, and they have a "spring" coiled above their back legs.

Why can't elephants jump?

Because of their shape, elephants can't bend enough to make a "spring" strong enough to jump.

Why do whales live longer than shrews?

You age with every heartbeat. Small animals' hearts beat very quickly, so they age more quickly than bigger animals.

Ideas for reading

Written by Clare Dowdall PhD
Lecturer and Primary Literacy Consultant

Learning objectives: read independently and with increasing fluency longer and less familiar texts; know how to tackle unfamiliar words that are not completely decodable; give some reasons why things happen; explain organizational features of texts, including alphabetical order, layout, diagrams, captions; explain ideas and processes using imaginative and adventurous vocabulary

Curriculum links: Science; History

Interest words: adapted, amoeba, ancestors, biologists, body weight, camouflage, evolution, famines, Galapagos, habitat, isolated, oxygen, predators, savannah, seep, spiracle, trachea

Word count: 1,317

Resources: whiteboard, ICT, internet

Getting started

- Read the title and ask children to suggest why they can't fly and what they think humans would need to have if they did, e.g. wings. Write their reasons on a whiteboard to return to later.

- Explain that this is a non-fiction book. Discuss what this means, and what features the children will find in it, e.g, contents and photographs with labels.

- Read through the glossary words, helping children to use a range of strategies to decode new words, e.g. phonics, awareness of familiar word parts and endings, breaking long words into syllables. Check that children can read the words that can't easily be decoded, e.g. amoeba.

Reading and responding

- Look at the contents together. Establish that this book is organized using a series of questions and that each chapter will attempt to answer the question about the features of different sorts of animals.

- Read pp2–3 together. Notice the use of the question as a title. Based on reading, discuss why birds can fly, but humans can't. Compare this information with their earlier predictions.

- Ask children to read to p27 in pairs, making brief notes that answer the questions raised by the book.